TO STAY OR TO LEAVE:- FORGIVING THE UNFORGIVABLE

DHANESH GHANASHYAM GAWDE

Copyright © Dhanesh Ghanashyam Gawde
All Rights Reserved.

ISBN 979-888569940-2

Contents

Preface

I said to the almond tree, "Friend, speak to me of God," and the almond tree blossomed.

To heal ourselves, we must first realise the role we played in our pain. Then we will be able to feel the pain and the sorrow of this realization, deeply and completely. Only then can we forgive and accept ourselves, allowing us to authentically forgive others. Out of this healing process, comes the clarity that gives us the answers we need to make the right decision and to fundamentally change.

FOREWORD

About the Author

He is Dhanesh Ghanashyam Gawde. He belongs from Goa but, he is completing his education in Sawantwadi, Sindhudurg. He is completing his education in Sawantwadi, Sindhudurg. He is currently doing BBI (Banking & Insurance) in Shri Pancham Khemraj College, Sawantwadi, Maharashtra. He is also done with Diploma of Computer Engineering. He likes to read and write stories, poems, qoutes, etc. He is very fond of writing horror stories too. His aim is to become a successful writer and author.

You can even follow him on his Instagram:- unreliableuniform62

Realization

The sick woman had asked to be brought to the workshop hoping to find a way to forgive her husband before she died. And then something else happened. Something she did not expect. She discovered that there was more to forgive than just her husband. There were two players in that drama called her life. Two principle actors. And she was one of the two. More than forgiving her husband, she needed to forgive herself.

With astounding clarity, she saw their silent pact for the life together. The choices they each had made and had lived by. Her husband's – to keep sleeping with other women, and hers – to stay with him anyway. He hadn't forced her to accept his choices. He hadn't forced her to live with him all these years. The choice to stay had always been her own. She had chosen to stay, and also to hate herself for staying. All her life, all her misery – was her own doing. It was as if a lightbulb had just gone on, altering everything she had believed to be true. Taking apart in an instant the elaborate, meticulously constructed story she had been telling herself all those years to protect herself from feeling the pain. Now, the dam was broken and nothing could stop the flood of feelings that rushed through her like a wild river.

There was too much to feel and too little time to feel it. Twenty-five years of hiding. Taking all that anger, all that desperate rage and stuffing it into her body, tucking it deep into her organs, away from her sight. They would lie there awaiting their time, petrifying into resentments, turning into cancerous cells, feeding on her relentless hate of herself, of her husband, of their life together. She had judged herself with more harshness and more determination than anyone else ever could. Did she have to be dying to let it be okay to love her husband? To finally take herself off the hook. She could never bring back of those years or undo what she had done. Sorrow-dark, wordless- the pain of the unforgivable- was lifting at the back of her throat threatening to choke her with its immensity of feelings... Overwhelming, but real, for the first time.

Feeling the Sorrow, Feeling the Pain

Sorrow is an emotion so profound it reaches the very depth of one's soul. It is the pain of the unforgivable in us, and it changes us forever. These are the skeletons in the burial places of our past. The skeletons that won't be buried. The things we did that we would do everything in our power to take back, and can't. The woman's sorrow: decades of self-recrimination and hate. Punishing herself, feeling worthless, lying to herself, denying, herself the right to love the man she loved, regardless of the circumstances... A quarter century of self-abuse. And then cancer.

The skeletons of the unforgivable. They roam the grounds in the night, keeping us awake, reminding us of what we did, and holding us prisoners. They need to be put to rest. They have rumbled too long. They, too, are tired and ready to be laid in the ground. "But how?" we ask. Again and again we try to lay them down, falling every time. After all, we have deemed them "The Unforgivable," and it seems beyond our power to simply let them be gone. How harshly we judge ourselves. How much easier it is at times to forgive another than oneself. How inventive we have become at the self-punishments we inflict. Keeping the pain alive, stirring the memories like embers of the fire that is never allowed to die out. And yet-it is pain that has opened our hearts to see others with the eyes of compassion and to be more understanding. Compassion is a caring born out of our sorrows, out of the tears we cry for things we cannot undo. Our sorrow is not determined by the severity of out crimes, but by the level of pain it has caused us and by how heavily we have judged ourselves for what we have done.

It could have been something minor, something someone else would have dismissed and forgotten long ago. To us, however, it is a source of continuous pain, a reminder of everything we hate about ourselves. I remember a fight. I had with my brother once. He must have been nine or ten years old. He was acting out, wanting something I wasn't letting him have. The details are gone. I can't remember a thing about that fight. But what I remember vividly, and what has turned into one of my most painful memories, is how I slammed the door of my car and drove off to work, knowing I wouldn't see him until the evening, wanting nothing else but to punish him in this way. His face filled with fear and pain and he was instantly sorry for what he had done. He saw I was ready to leave and had wanted to rush to me and make up. We were very close and I knew he wanted to apologize and not let me go like this... but his friend was there watching the scene, and so he held himself back-acted like it didn't matter. I saw all this is an instant, but would not relent... and so I slammed that car door and drove off. My day was ruined, of course, and when I came home from work in the evening, we made up, and everything went on as usual.

What was the big deal? I am sure my brother would not even remember that fight. He probably forgot about it the next day. It was one of so many we had at the time. As for me, it is difficult to write about it even now. I have tried to forgive myself for it endless times. Sometimes, I remember that morning, without the usual tension in my stomach that accompanies it. But I did feel it now, while writing about it. That memory is one of my sorrows. Something I did that I can never take back. Made stronger by the significance I gave it. For me – it meant I was not a good enough brother. For me – nothing was worse than that. We are our own severest judges. Giving ourselves life sentences for things for which we would easily forgive others. Yes, I know sorrow well. It's been my dark companion for a great number of years. But not everything we regret doing will become our sorrow. There are things I did in my past that were certainly far more serious than the fight with my brother. Many of them became my life lessons, but not my sorrows. I have felt remorse. I regret the circumstances, but I am not really sorry. It is a paradox, and it is the truth. A part of me knows innately that these incidents had to play out that way. I am sorry for the pain I caused others, but not sorry I did what I did. Out of the rubble of those experiences, as I emerged that eventually became what I am today. Would it have been better to learn the same lessons differently?

Perhaps, but I didn't. And I forgave myself for them. That past has no hold on me, and I am richer for having lived it. There are other things in my life that have turned into my sorrows. Most I've been able to put to rest. Some are still not quite gone, though their voices grow fainter and fainter as my heart heals and I forgive myself at deeper levels. I know the day will come, and it will be soon, that these memories will lose their hold on me. One day they will fade away forever. I will be free. Not everybody carries sorrows in their hearts. To some, forgiveness of self comes easily. It is part of their grace. They have an ability to feel remorse and then to simplify let go. Some have a gift, a natural ease with self-forgiveness. Some don't. And then, there comes the forgiveness of others.

Forgiving the Unforgivable

Forgiveness, We give so much life service to this word, using it casually and often without real understanding, thus making it less attainable, stripping it of the immensity of its power. Forgive we say, often without thinking. I can never forgive, we say just as often. Not realizing that by saying this, we are giving a silent consent for pain to lodge itself deeper and deeper into our psyche. As long as there are people in our past we have not forgiven, we are not free of them. They are with us at all times, forever close, breathing down our necks, whispering into our ears, mocking us, threatening our peace of mind, a constant conscious or unconscious reminder of our pain. If you were to stop and think about it for a moment, aren't there people from your recent past or from times long gone with whom you are having silent dialogues? Arguing, proving your point, fighting back, never succeeding in being heard, always ending the conversation angrier and more frustrated than when you started? Thus keeping the conflict that might have happened twenty or thirty years ago as fresh and alive as if what had caused it happened yesterday?

The father you have forgiven for what he did to you when you were a junior in high school – he is right here, looking over your shoulder, telling you'll never amount to anything. Just like he did when you were seventeen. But I haven't seen him or spoken to him in twenty years! Doesn't matter. He is still here. You have not let him go. And everyone in authority over you, real or perceived, becomes "The Father," the one who would never approve, the one who would always bring you down, the one you need to rebel against, or seek acceptance from or both. And what's most frightening – you don't even know it. And now you are thirty seven, a father yourself, still having problems with authority figures, fathers, all of them. You are not free to respond to them as an adult. Instead, you are at the mercy of unconscious reflexes, an adolescent in a body of a grown up man. Yes, we carry the ones we won't forgive on our backs, whether we know it or not. And only forgiveness will bring an end to it. "But if I were to forgive," some say, "Then I will forget what they did to me. And I never want to forgive that. There are things that were done to me that I can never forgive. Never ever. I won't forgive them. I can't."

I understand. Murder, rape, incest, physical and emotional abuse, cruelty to children... the list is long. The list is endless. That's true. And here lies the paradox of forgiveness. These truly are things that appears to be unforgivable, and yet we must forgive to be free of them. Advocates of the death penalty, and those friends and relatives of the victims who are sure that witnessing the death of the murderer will bring them a measure of release from the pain of their loss, have discovered that this is not so. The completion they had hoped to find did not come with the death of the one who took the life of their loved ones. In many cases, it was simply the end of the first phase of their grief. The only way they could cope with the tragedy was to focus all their energy on justice. Finding the murderer, wishing for the death sentence, watching the unfolding of court proceedings – anything, anything at all that could take them away from fully feeling the unimaginable horror of their loss. To feel that would be to die themselves. Often they wished for that, often their pain was more than they could bear. That initial phase of grief, lasting at times for many years, would keep the survivors of the tragedy locked in their bottomless anger, wishing for revenge, fighting for it, hoping, believing that only revenge, once it happens, would bring relief to the unutterable pain they were living with every day. And then the execution takes place, the murderer's life is taken, but the hoped for completion does not come. Instead, there is an emptiness that does not alleviate the pain, but brings it more to the surface. An emptiness the survivors did not expect. Nothing has changed. The pain is as strong as ever-maybe stronger-because there is nothing there anymore to distract them from feeling it. In some cases, this becomes a doorway to finally being able to feel the immensity of their loss, followed by a degree of healing, perhaps even forgiveness and change. There are also those who remain locked in their pain, nursing the hate for the ones who caused it and thus staying connected to them (dead or alive) for the rest of their lives.

"But I have every night to hate them! Don't tell me not to hate! Don't talk to me about forgiveness! I am right! And I know it. I will hate them as long as I live!" Yes. You have every right to hate them. And if you do, they have not just taken from you the life of the one you loved, they have also effectively taken yours. The healing of your pain cannot happen with the fulfillment of your dream for revenge. But it will happen with forgiveness. Once you consciously take your energy away from hate, you may at first experience disorientation. This is what happens as one is about to come out of their grief. In essence, it is a kind of letting go, like opening a tightly held fist and releasing the pain – not to forget it, but to be free from it. You may not even be aware of having forgiven the one who took what was everything in your life away from you. But there is no familiar gripping in the pit of your stomach when you think about that person. Now even his image is fading and drifting away. You think about the one you lost, and you know nothing will ever take this love away. You will never forget what happened to you. How can you? Your loss has become part of you and it has changed you forever. It has changed the direction of your life, but it doesn't have to define you. You have you had- it is gone. But there is a different future that can be yours. A depth of soul, a level of compassion and with it-a new light. Your loss is woven into the fabric of your being, and yet-you are free from its hold on you. We don't have to forgive what was done to us, if we can't. We may never forgive that. But we must forgive the why of what they did. The famous words of Jesus Christ: "Forgive them, father, for they know not what they do" is a phenomenal example of a great soul forgiving the unforgivable. What does it mean to forgive the why of what was done to us, even if at times we can't forgive the what? Most will agree people are not born monsters. Yet, sometimes, they turn into one. Things happen to them in the course of their lives. Bad things. Terrible things. Pain gets inflicted, causing rage, humiliation, hurt, shame. Often it is not so much what happened to them, but how they dealt with it. Some are better equipped to deal with pain than others. The same event in the same family may turn one brother into a criminal, while the other will go on to become a great humanitarian teacher. It is not for us to judge the effect of the experience on another human being. We are all different, and so are our abilities to cope and the choices we make. The fact that people have suffered crippling emotional or physical pain, causing damage they have not found a way to heel, does not then give them a license to continue to perpetrate the same or worse crimes upon others. But understanding these causes helps us forgive the "Why" of their behavior.

Jesus calls on the Father to forgive his torturers while in the grips of unimaginable pain.

Why?

Because he has a profound understanding that those who did it to him, did it out of their own pain, ignorance and fear. Their own souls had been damaged by what had been done to them. That's what made them capable of such cruelty only forgiveness has the power to break this chain of pain. To refuse to forgive is to always live a slave to our impulses. The dark impulses born out of our rage and shame out of our hate and self-hatred. Jesus became a teacher of a different way of being: turn the other cheek, forgive, walk away. And humanity has been struggling with the concept ever since. But I am greatly moved by the story of Jesus Christ. It matters not whether you believe these were actual events or simply mythology. There isn't a powerful example of a call for forgiveness and of the explanation for the reason to do it.

Forgiveness is a State of Grace

Certain misconceptions about forgiveness make it harder to understand it. Some view forgiveness as weakness others are unwilling to forgive out of fear that they would have to resume a relationship with the people they have forgiven, something they have no intention or interest in doing. Neither of these assumptions is true. The only reason to forgive is to set yourself free of your past, so you can step into the myriad of available futures that you can't see through the eyes of pain. Forgiveness swings open the door to the Power of the Possible and delivers you to the other side. There, on the other side of forgiveness, the most unimaginable scenarios lie waiting for you to show up and claim. You've stepped through the looking glass and anything is possible. On the other side of forgiveness, your sight is clearer, your perceptions uncluttered. The people you used to hate may surprise you with kindnesses, or leave your life so utterly, you'll wonder if you didn't just dream your past. You may also discover there is more to forgive than just them. You may discover, that the person you need to forgive most is yourself. Forgiveness is a state of grace. I said it earlier, but it bears repeating: Forgiveness cannot be done, but only received. It is, in a sense, our rain dance for freedom. When it doesn't rain in the desert, the natives dance. They dance "a rain dance" so that it will rain. And then, at some point-it does. Does it rain because they danced? Would it have rained even if they hadn't? "Of course," we say. The weather does not depend on a dance. Maybe so. But does it matter? They dance anyway. They dance so that it will rain and then it does. We take the steps to forgive, we dance the dance of forgiveness, and then at some point what we used to feel about that particular person-we don't feel anymore. It is simply gone. How did it happen? I have tried to forgive many times, but every time I did I would just clench my teeth and my stomach would get tense and I would need a glass of water and then the telephone would ring and then I would have to deal with things... and I just couldn't... it was the same every time. But I kept trying. Just like I was supposed to... and then one day, or one night, as I cried myself to sleep one more time... I just don't know what happened... I woke up different. I looked for my anger and it was gone. The hate? I hadn't had a minute it as long as I could remember. Where was it? Gone. You look for it all the familiar places, you bring back familiar images, images that used to make you cringe, but they don't make you feel the way they did in the past. Now it is like watching a cartoon. They have lost their power, and you simply turn them off. What happened? When? When was it taken? Does it matter? Maybe your intention was all that was needed. Forgiveness comes from the realm of the miraculous. It's a magic that cannot be put into the words of our language. It defies our logic; it is beyond our intellectual understanding. Whatever we believed we understand about its mechanism doesn't begin to touch it.

Forgiveness is a gift.

Once we experienced it, once we are touched by it, its grace changes us forever. A cancer, spread through the body of a dying woman-gone in an instant. A miracle? Absolutely. But a true story never-the-less. It is one of many. Not as many as we would like, but it did happen. And if one crow is white then not all crows are black. She went on to live a life she had never let herself live before. She saw the truth of her situation, she felt her pain-and she forgave herself. Forgave herself. Forgave herself for all the years of self-loathing and self-depreciating hatred. And then she gave herself permission to live the life she choose. For the first time ever, she didn't need permission from anyone else. And she forgave her husband. She saw him in all his complexity and she just let it him be. And it was okay to love him and to stay with even if he would never be faithful. Her choice to live, propelled by the power of her acceptance of herself, was all it took.

Accepting Yourself

There is tremendous power in accepting yourself. And yet, the very concept remains foreign to most people. It is not something we are taught as children growing up. Not at school, not at home, not anywhere. Maybe because those who are supposed to teach us not to demand perfection of ourselves, to be forgiving and kind to ourselves, to have the patience and the understanding that making mistakes is part of what makes us human – don't know it themselves. So many cultures are based on the demand for perfection. A demand that can never be attained, but is never-the-less ingrained into the very fabric of our being, having been spoon-fed to us since we were born. By the time we can walk and say our first words, it is already done. We know it is not okay to make mistakes. And when we do – we will be severely punished for them. No wonder we grow up to become our own worst judges, refusing ourselves the compassion. We may willingly extend to strangers. There are 4 main principles of self-acceptance. These principles, once mastered, can make the difference between a life of continuous self judgement, self-punishment and blame and a life of reflection and understanding, deeply rooted in compassion and healing of the heart. Print them out, put them on your bathroom mirror or any place. You can see them every day. Read them again and again. Make them an integral part of your being.

Four Principles of Self-Acceptance

1. Realize that you are a human being and as such you can and will make mistakes. (It is not a crime to make mistakes, it is simply a fact of life.)

2. For these mistakes – you can be forgiven. And you can forgive.

3. Sometimes you are prepared for life and sometimes you are not. And that's how it will always be. (This means that there are and will be situations in your life where things will happen, for which you will not be prepared. And so you might act in ways that, had you been better prepared, you would not have acted. It doesn't mean that you are a bad person. Again, it is just – a fact of life. You can be forgiven for these actions, and you can forgive yourself).

4. Your needs and wants are important, though they may not be the first priority. That they are not the first priority does not mean they are not important. They matter. You matter. You are important. Stop here for a second. Let these words sink in: you matter. You are important. When I heard this, the first time many years ago, it turned my world upside down. Such a simple statement. Such an obvious thing. Why then was I sobbing? I didn't even know that I thought I didn't matter before. I simply never thought about it. So many things mattered to me. My family, my business.... But myself? Wasn't it selfish? To think about yourself? To make myself important? I am aware that some may read this and shrug. If you were raised to love yourself – great. You have been lucky. But in our world today, sadly you are a minority. I learned the principles of self-acceptance years ago, and understanding them was one of the turning points of my life. To me – they were a revelation. I could be forgiven? It was actually okay to make mistakes? And not just that. It was a given that I would make them again? I never thought about it in the past. I simply knew I had to be punished. And if not by others, then by myself. The harsher – the better. A mechanism that started soon after birth and had become an innate part of me. It took me years to undo it. It is something I still remind myself of at times. I hope the day will come when self-acceptance will become for me as automatic as punishing myself had been for so long. There are times when it already is. The dying woman

in the story had an epiphany. In deep meditative state, saw herself in a way she had never allowed herself before. And she accepted herself with all her vulnerabilities. She let it be okay to stay with her husband even if he was never going to be faithful to her. She let it be okay to love him anyway. So profound was her acceptance of herself that the self-forgiveness was its natural by product. So profound was her awakening to the truth of herself, that the wave of self- love that washed through her body dissolved the cancerous cells in that very instant.

Making the Right Decision

The right decision is a decision that is right for you. Not for your friends, not for your parents or your children and not for anyone else. What's right for you, really right, will also in the end be right for others. But you must know what it is first. Thinking and using logic and reason alone won't get you there. Nor will the usual substitutes for the real feelings: self-pity, avoidance, resentments, denial and blame. And you will be stuck in indecision for years, or make a decision for you may later regret, never quite certain it was the right one. Or lie to yourself about what you really want, just like the woman in the story, refusing to feel until an inch away from death. She had an awakening in the last minute, and she had a miraculous healing. Not everyone does. I know it is scary to look inside and discover what you really feel, especially if you have been avoiding it all your life. But there is no way around it. You must lift out of the entanglement of your feelings, so you can see clearly.

One way to go about getting in touch with what you really feel is to write a letter addressed, for example, to your partner. It will be a letter that you will not mail. Write it and make it real for you. It doesn't have to be fair or right or justified. The only reason to do it, is to get it all out. If that's what's inside, you want to be free from it, so it doesn't continue to poison you. If you feel too sorry for yourself and just want to stop; write just that, and keep on writing. Don't evaluate what you write, don't analyze it, don't pay attention to grammar or punctuation and just keep going. At a certain point your walls will break down, you will drop the pretense and the real you will come out. Remember: this is a letter no one will see. You will not mail it. But it is your ticket to freedom. So write. And as you hand moves down the paper, everything you hold inside will start flowing out. Don't let your tears stop the writing. You want to feel it all. Only then can you get to a neutral place-the only place from which to make a decision. Once you are done with the writing and there is nothing more to add-fold the letter and put it away for a day. MAKE SURE that no one finds this letter. You don't want anyone to come across it and read it. Ever. Especially someone mentioned in the letter. This could be a very hurtful and punishing thing, and it may be very damaging to your relationship.

Next day-re-read the letter slowly, add to it or make corrections to make it stronger. Then fold it and put it away again. On the third day, re-read what you have written one more time, slowly, without adding anything. After that, BURN THE LETTER page by page. This is very important. You are giving your subconscious mind a clear message: *I am letting go of this anger. I am done with it.* Having worked with many people to whom I had given this technique, I have discovered that burning the letter sooner than three days doesn't work. One girl told me that she had experienced great difficulty burning the pages even on the second day. "Was it because the fire would keep dying, or because it was hard for you to do it emotionally?" I asked. "It was not the fire," she said. "It was me. I felt tremendous resistance. I just didn't want to burn these pages." Yes, holding on to angers has many pay offs; blaming, being right, self-pity, righteous anger to name a few. And while they may not feel good, many keep taking these pay offs because they are as addictive as any drug-addictive and very dangerous, often leading to a serious or fatal illness. Trying to answer what may be the most difficult question in your life while avoiding feeling the pain that this is causing you is like trying to see through fogged glass: everything is blurred. The answers you are seeking lie on the other side of the wall of your feelings. This wall will melt and dissolve once you allow the feelings to flow. If we were to liken our emotions to a deep pool of water, the answers to our questions wait for us at the bottom of this pool. You must find the strength to step into that pool and then to dive in. Try the following visualization: imagine yourself a scuba diver wearing an oxygen mask and all the necessary equipment, so you can breathe under the water. Begin to slowly float down, towards the bottom of this pool of emotions. Now-forget about everything else, and focus on what you are feeling. Imagine the things that are causing you pain and let yourself feel what comes with all the intensity you can muster.

At first you will probably feel anger. Anger is usually so close to the surface, that it is easy to tap into. Anger may switch to hurt, then to more anger, then back to hurt. You may come upon rage, fear, sadness, shame, sorrow, remorse. Feel them, and let them go. Right, wrong, justified, unjustified, easy or hard... stay with them and keep sinking deeper. Resist the urge to get the help out of the pool. That's what you've done every time in the past. When it felt like too much. That's why you are so clogged, searching for answers and never finding them. Do it differently this time. Have the guts to stay with your feelings no matter how difficult it is and how scared you are. The deeper you go-the more you will find. And not more pain-more beauty. The most beautiful emotions have substance and weight. They don't float on the surface or in the upper layers of the pool. Love, hope, happiness, joy, forgiveness, peace... they all are waiting for you on the way to the bottom. You can't get to them without first wading through everything else that's in your way. They also hold your answers. Too many times, having made it almost to the bottom, a voice whispers in your ear; that's too much, you can't take it anymore. This is a voice that has led you down the wrong path every time. A voice of your negative ego, an enemy inside you. But instead of dismissing this voice, the voice that has never ever told you the truth, you respond to it and rush all the way up, back to the surface. Not reaching the bottom, not finding the freedom, not finding the release. There was just one minute left. Maybe even a second, no more... but you didn't trust what you knew. You allowed yourself, once again, to be seduced by your ego. And instead of coming up cleansed, pushed upwards into the clean, fresh air of knowing, you experienced a partial release only and are still left without the answer you sought. Think about it. Isn't it fascinating? Why is feeling pain so terribly frightening to people that they will go to any length to avoid it? Let me give you another example of this.

A young man who was sick with cancer was working with a psychotherapist. Sometimes he would come to the therapy sessions with his mother, often too weak after his chemotherapy treatment. Knowing that at the root of every physical illness lies emotional cause, the therapist was trying to help the young man's father had died years before and that the son had never grieved his death. "Next time, when you come, why don't I help you get through your feelings, so you can grieve you dad's death," the doctor suggested. The young man's body stiffened. He looked at his feet, folded his arms across his chest. He reached for the glass of water. The therapist waited. "No," the man broke the silence. "No. I'd rather keep doing chemotherapy. I only vomit for four hours after the chemo. I can deal with that." And yet, frightening or not, feelings are simply that feelings. They fluctuate and they change-high-tide, low-tide, storms, fires, droughts. Small children before they've learned to adapt and to imitate adults are a good example. Crying one moment, laughing happily the next. Feelings come and go. Teach yourself how not to stuff them. Feel them, and release them, so you can be free. Because as long as they are in the way, you will be run by them. And eventually – destroyed by them. Unexpressed, unattended constricting feelings are the time bombs ready to explode. The clock is set, but the time is unknown.

At the root of cancer lies anger, old, petrified, unexpressed, and now deadly. It is the anger that we are sure is too late to do anything about. There is nothing I can do about it, it happened too long ago, it is too late now is the messages we give our subconscious again and again. Sometimes the anger may indeed be so old, we don't even remember it. We have succeeded in tucking it away, hiding it even from ourselves. But it is there, as alive and potent as when it was first born, and it is doing its deadly job. The subconscious gets the message: it is too late. The subconscious does not judge or evaluate. It simply follows the given program. The body follows as well. It is too late. And a person gets a deadly illness. Designed to get him out of here because it is too late for here. It is not too late! And this bomb slowly ticking away inside often can be stopped. So many have done it successfully. None of them without getting to the bottom of their feelings and freeing themselves from their constructing grip. Having a life threatening illness was their motivation. It doesn't have to go that far. Self-pity, being sorry for yourself, is not a feeling, but a mood, a condition. It is an anesthetic that keeps you stuck, and so does blaming-yourself or others. They are the "drugs" to alleviate pain, and just as addictive. The drugs that don't heal you but kill you instead. Killing you slowly, or on the spot, like an overdose. With a heart attack or a cancer or a severe depression.

What is depression? Imagine gauze like strips of anger laid upon each other one layer at a time. A slow process, building up with the years, eventually creating a thick, impenetrable brick, hard and dark and solid, that is now pressing onto your chest. Composed of all your angers, big and small, gathered over the years. All of them-unattended, stuffed together, so many it is impossible to pick apart. And you are doing nothing about it. Just letting they build. Until one morning you can't get out of bed, and you can't explain why. Or something very minor happens-a colleague at the next desk at work laughs too loud, again (!!!!) after you've asked her so many times not to... and you can't take it anymore. That was the last straw. You snap. You see no point in living. That's depression. Now you are a prime candidate for real drugs-antidepressants which you hope will make you feel better. But they will do nothing to take away the original cause. The rate of cancer is increasing. Depression is on the rise. More and more, we hear of people dying of heart attacks in the prime of life. An athlete, a young man who seemed to have nothing wrong with his health at all, suddenly drops dead on a tennis court. A heart attack at the age of forty. But there was nothing wrong with his heart before?! Are you sure? What determines whether or not something was wrong with one's heart? Does heartache qualify? A heartache that is not measurable by means of traditional medicine? But men must be strong they must "bear it like a man," ignore the pain of heart and keep "handling it."

Do they?

In many cases, the first symptom of a heart attack is death. Happening to people too young to die. What's going on? A heart too full of pain can bear only so much. And it gives up. If you are in medical profession and are reading this, don't dismiss it too readily. Don't dismiss the increasing number of healings that defy medical explanations either. I have great respect for our western medicine. My friend's life was saved at least twice when she had internal bleedings that she was not aware of until too much blood had been lost. Why was she bleeding internally? Bleeding high up in her stomach, so close to the heart? What was it that she couldn't stomach? I will tell you the truth. She couldn't stomach the fact that her marriage (her first marriage) was unraveling and she felt powerless to stop the avalanche. We were losing what we once had with each other, becoming strangers under the same roof, and she had no tools to deal with what was happening. And so she did what most people do.

She cried, she fought, she withdrew into hostile silences, she punished, she blamed, and she felt very sorry for herself. Yet, she never permitted herself to just fall apart in a real way. To drop to the very bottom of my pain and face the truth. It wasn't anyone's fault. It worked when we were very young, but it couldn't work long term, she wasn't ready for this truth. She wasn't ready to even consider leaving the marriage. She bled instead. Wonderful doctors in the emergency rooms saved her, stopped the bleeding in time, and she didn't die. But in the end, it was the emotional healing, the healing of heart, the healing of the pain that had caused the bleeding that brought this to an end. And the bleedings stopped. Our emotions have tremendous power. They have the power of life and death. When you are faced with a decision that will profoundly change the direction of your life, a decision that will affect the lives of others close to you. A decision that will affect all of your family in the deepest way, so much lies in the balance. So important it is to make the right choice. A choice that is right for you. The one you will not question in the future. A decision that, looking back, you will know was the right thing to do. No matter how difficult and painful it was, it eventually brought healing to everyone it had affected. When you are making a decision of this magnitude, you need to have all of yourself present. You're thinking and you feeling, your intellect and your heart. You need to find the right balance between your love and your will. Your will-that strength and power without you to do what needs to be done, difficult or not. And your love, the part of you that wants to follow your heart whether or not it is the right thing to do. You need to find the balance between them. Freedom is not simple and not always comfortable. There is a responsibility that comes with it. A responsibility to make the right choices. A responsibility to not consciously hurt another with our choices.

The answers we seek come with our understanding of this complexity. Each one of us is a synergy of so many ports. We each carry the light and we also carry the darkness. We are familiar with our darkness. It is our light that scares us. At times we are filled with the most gracious giving. At other times we can be distant and cold and unavailable. We can be monsters and we can be saints. We can be everything, and often we are.

The more healing we have experienced, the stronger is our choice to act out of our beauty and not out of our negativity. To look for a simple answer, a "yes" or a "no" to a complex situation, is to not respect yourself. You deserve more than that. Give yourself the space you need. Honor yourself in this way. Once you've told yourself the truth, once you've let yourself feel all the feelings you've been holding in check for so long, once you've accepted and forgiven yourself and accepted the facts of your situation without embellishing them or making them worse than they are, the answers you are looking for simply be there, and you will just know. For some it is right to end the relationship, for others it is right to stay. There is no right or wrong answer. It is what's right for you. Don't rush this process. Don't skip the steps. Have the courage to do what it takes. So you can be free. Otherwise, no matter you decide, there will be regret, there will be sorrow, and there will be doubt. At the level of choice, magic enters one's life- magic that shows us the Power of the Possible and our true magnificence. It takes courage to step that far. To let yourself see that light in yourself. Not many have that level of courage. Be the one who does. Let your life shine the light on the life of others. If one can do it, so can many. Why not you?